ENNISKILLEN

For N.M.H. and P.W.W.

This book has received financial support from the Cultural Traditions
Programme of the Community Relations Council which aims to encourage
acceptance and understanding of cultural diversity.

Friar's Bush Press
24 College Park Avenue
BELFAST BT7 1LR
Published 1990
© Copyright reserved
ISBN 0 946872 31 7

Designed by Rodney Miller Associates, Belfast
Printed by W. & G. Baird, Antrim

ENNISKILLEN
Historic Images of an Island Town

Helen Lanigan Wood

FRIAR'S BUSH PRESS

The capture of Maguire's Enniskillen Castle in 1593/94 by the Elizabethan army. Illustrated by the English soldier John Thomas, this drawing shows the sparsely inhabited countryside where the town of Enniskillen was to be built. On the right is "Captaine Bingham's Campe", on the site of the West Battery, locally called The Redoubt. "The governers battle" on the left is on the site of the East Battery, known locally as The Forthill.

4

EARLY DAYS

The town of Enniskillen was established by a charter of King James 1 in 1612. This was part of a major new scheme of colonisation - known as the Plantation of Ulster - of the counties of Donegal, Londonderry, Tyrone, Armagh, and Cavan as well as Fermanagh. An important part of this well planned scheme was the creation of eighteen borough towns such as Enniskillen which would be represented in the Dublin parliament.

Much thought was given to choosing suitable sites for the corporate towns. In Fermanagh the Lord Deputy, Arthur Chichester and the Attorney-General, Sir John Davies, initially opted for the idyllic setting of the Franciscan abbey at Lisgoole before deciding in favour of the island where stood the ruins of Enniskillen Castle. The castle had been built in the early 15th century by the Maguires, Gaelic chieftains who had ruled Fermanagh for over 300 years until dispossessed after the Elizabethan wars.The island site could be defended easily and the new town would have the advantage of an already existing castle. With this decision began the gradual transformation over the next three or more centuries of the rolling hills of Enniskillen into an urban landscape leaving undisturbed across the waters of Lough Erne, scarcely a mile distant, the rural tranquillity that still prevails at Lisgoole.

The responsibility for establishing the new town was given to William Cole, a Londoner, who had served with the crown forces in Ireland and had been appointed constable of Enniskillen castle in 1609. By a series of complicated grants and agreements in 1611 and the following year, including an exchange of land already granted to him near Enniskillen, Cole had become by May 1612 the sole owner of all sixty acres of Enniskillen island. His descendants, the Earls of Enniskillen, were to reap the benefits by becoming landlords of the whole town.

The town was to be built on twenty acres on the east side and additional land was to be set aside off the island, to the east, for burgage tenements and a commons for cattle owned by the townspeople.

On February 27th 1612 (1613 according to the new Gregorian calendar of 1582 observed by the Irish) the establishment of the town was formalised in King James' charter. William Cole was nominated as provost or " sovereign" of the new borough and fourteen burgesses were appointed to the Corporation. Three months later the new Dublin parliament opened and "Inishkillin" borough was represented there by Roger Atkinson and Humphry Farnham.

William Cole set about his new duties with energy. He rebuilt the ruined castle, erected a house for his family just outside its walls, and built wooden bridges at the east and west ends of the island. He brought over British settlers with skills to build houses and all the public buildings needed for the borough. He provided building materials at his own expense, timber and raw materials for making clay roof tiles and three hundred thousand bricks. Examples of these early Enniskillen-made bricks and roof tiles were found in 1990 during archaeological excavations near the site of Cole's house.

Not all necessities could be obtained locally. As late as 1655, Cole was importing corn and other goods from London through the Donegal port of Killybegs and in 1647 such items as buttons, combs, broadcloth, sword belts and hats were imported from London for Cole's regiment in Enniskillen.

The name Enniskillen comes from the Irish *inis* (island) and *Cethlenn,* the genitive case of *Ceithle,* but scholars do not agree on the meaning of *Ceithle.* According to the Annals of Clonmacnoise, which survives only in a 17th century English translation, *Loway Keyhleann (of whom Iniskihlean took the name)* was a king of the legendary Tuatha De Danann for forty years. According to another source - the Annals of the Four Masters Cethlenn wounded the Dagda at the Battle of Moytura, and John O 'Donovan in a footnote to this passage states that

A View of Enniskillen taken from the Forthill 1787

a East Bridge
b Session House
c Meeting house
d White Hart Inn
e Market house
f Water Lane
g Factory houses

h Bleach yard
i School house
k Bason
l Convent
m Church
n Church Yard
o Castle

The key buildings of the town are shown in this sketch of 1787 by William Clarke. In the centre is the Market House(c) built about 1746. Nearby between two large "factory houses"(g) is a bleach yard(h) where brown linen, produced extensively in Fermanagh at the time, could be bleached. The "convent"(l) was probably a Franciscan friary. In the troubled year of 1689 the friars were obliged to leave the town, but probably returned later. Close to it is the Free School(i) endowed by a Royal Charter in 1617 with over 2000 acres of land. In 1777, the Royal School was transferred to its present site at Portora.

Cethlenn, according to old accounts of the battle, was a woman and wife of Balor, leader of the legendary Formorian tyrants.

The story is further complicated by a tradition going back to at least the 18th century that the name *Inis Cethlenn* referred to a tiny islet beside the East Bridge, after which the larger island and the town were named. A more likely explanation, however, is that the town was called after Enniskillen Castle, as there are numerous references to the Maguire Castle of *Inis Cethlenn* in 15th and 16th century entries in the Annals.

None of the early town buildings have survived. The original parish church was the medieval church of St Fergus on Inniskeen Island, but by 1622 work had begun on a new church in Enniskillen on the site of the present St Macartin's Cathedral. In 1649 the first Presbyterian meeting house was built. In 1622 Cole had gathered together £500 or £600 to build a Session House. It included a gaol and was built on the site of the present Court House.

Enniskillen played an important part in the Williamite Wars of 1689-90, supporting the cause of King William. The two famous regiments of the town - The Royal Inniskilling Dragoons and The Royal Inniskilling Fusiliers - originated in regiments raised at that time. Ironically the town survived the turmoil of these years relatively unscathed but disaster struck in 1695 when an accidental fire destroyed most of the houses. The town had barely recovered from this blow when another dreadful fire occurred in 1705 leaving 114 families homeless. Appeals went out all over Ireland and England to help the victims and the response was such that the town was able to be rebuilt. Some of the appeal funds may have been used to purchase the fine Queen Anne mace made for the town in Dublin in 1707-8.

In the 17th and 18th centuries the town remained small, the houses modest in scale. In 1739 when Dean Henry visited Enniskillen there were only about 150 houses and *most of these indifferent cabins*. A hundred years later the number of houses had grown to over a thousand, but almost two thirds of them were thatched, a factor no doubt contributing to the frequent fires.

As the 18th century progressed, Enniskillen became increasingly prosperous with thriving fairs and markets and a growing linen industry. By the middle of the century the most impressive building was probably the Market House built about 1746 on the central Diamond where trade and commerce were concentrated.

The linen industry at this time was a cottage industry. Flax was grown locally and cloth was woven in their own homes by part-time farmers. The work of preparing the yarn - spinning, boiling and winding - provided employment for women. The products were brought to Enniskillen where there were separate markets for flax, yarn, and various kinds of linen cloth, coarse and fine, bleached and unbleached. Bleaching was a separate enterprise and the site of one such operation near the Diamond in Enniskillen is shown on Clarke's drawing of the town in 1787. The heyday of these markets was the mid to late 18th century interrupted by a general slump in the 1770's. In the second quarter of the 19th century this cottage industry declined, overtaken by the advent of power looms.

There was also a small and short-lived cotton industry established in 1785 by the Earl of Enniskillen in co-operation with two men called Marshall and Cochrane. Among its products were corduroy, velveteen and quilting. Ten houses were built in Beggar (now Henry) Street to accommodate both looms and families of workers, while other looms were housed in the centre of the town near an associated carding and spinning factory. The raw cotton for this industry was, of course, all imported. Even when industries like this one declined, Enniskillen was able to maintain a relatively stable economy through the good agricultural economy of its hinterland, which in the 18th century was based largely on cattle rather than on cereal production.

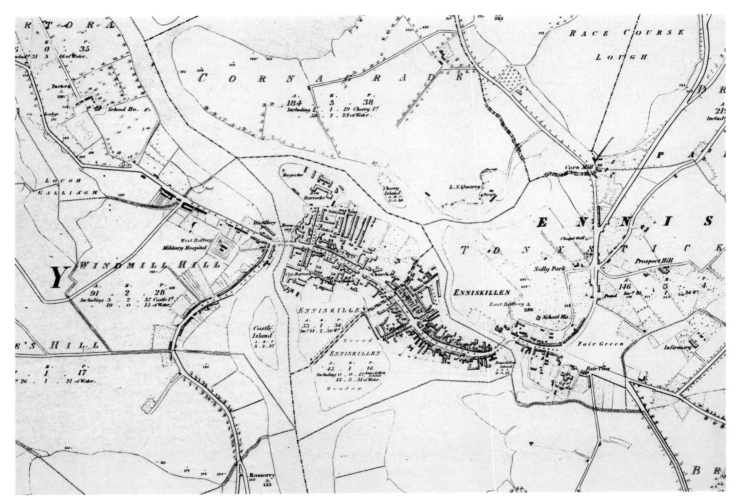

Ordnance Survey map of Enniskillen in 1834. Many old street names are recorded here - Gaol street (now Belmore Street), Main Street (now divided between East Bridge and Townhall Streets), Barrack Street (now Queen Street), and Beggar Street (now Henry Street). The old name of the Hollow is marked, a name still widely used by local people but replaced officially by High Street and Church Street. Further to the west is Brook Street always known locally as The Brook and near the centre of the town is the old area of Boston - an unusual name of obscure origin.

Enniskillen Castle and Watergate c.1826. In the 1820s the military barracks beside the castle was still being extended to provide additional accommodation. An army plan of 1822 shows that the building immediately behind the Watergate served as a store and armoury while the lean-to shed outside it housed "privies". The crenellated wall protecting the west side of the castle was later incorporated in a two storied building accommodating hospital and barracks above gunsheds and stables. On the right is the Church of Ireland Parish Church (later St Macartin's Cathedral) without its spire which had deteriorated so badly that it had to be taken down a few years earlier. (Drawing by R. O'Callaghan Newenham)

A view of the town from the north west - Portora Hill - in 1837. In the left foreground a Lough Erne cot with a mast and sail unburdens its cargo. On the hill to the right is the West Battery or Redoubt. During the Elizabethan Wars Captain George Bingham attacked the castle from this vantage point, and in 1688 an earthen fort was built here to protect the western approach to the town. In 1796 this fort was either replaced or rebuilt and was enclosed in 1829 by a parapet wall. The Barracks Hospital, seen here on the skyline, was built in the same year. Smoke from the high chimney beside the west bridge denotes a busy distillery, owned by Robert Thompson in 1817, contrasting with the smokeless chimney of his other distillery near the barracks which was put on the market in 1833. (Print by J.H. Burgess)

A panoramic view of the town from the south west about 1860. The Church of Ireland Parish Church with its fine spire dominates the western end of the town. Below it to the south west is the Roman Catholic Chapel built in 1802-3 and renovated in 1825. The parishioners numbered 1500 and they had to stand during Sunday Mass. The only seating was a form provided by Lord Thomas Maguire for himself and his son Denis. The present St Michael's Church opened in 1875. At the east end of the town is the recently completed monument in memory of Sir Galbraith Lowry Cole, distinguished General in the Peninsular Wars against Napoleon and a descendant of the founder of Enniskillen. (Lithograph by Newman & Co. London)

When this Townhall was completed in 1812, replacing an earlier market house, it contained a large hall for public meetings, a savings bank, a court for the recovery of small debts and a marshalsea. The steeple, which had been added in 1782 to the mid 18th century house, was retained and used as an office. The barred windows of the marshalsea, a prison for debtors and their goods, can be seen next to the steeple on the first floor. On fair days the Diamond and the ground floor of the market house were thronged with stalls selling fruit, vegetables, fish, haberdashery and earthenware. In this photograph of c.1897 the haberdashery stall in the foreground is manned by Johnny Tuthill and the vigilant policeman is Constable Reilly. The man closest to Roberts' shop is the butcher John O'Donnell who also appears on page 39. (Mercer photograph)

THE TOWN DEVELOPS

Linen was Fermanagh's main export in the 18th century, but in the 19th century, farm produce, in particular butter was to overtake it in importance. At this period the town's butter market, held every Monday and Tuesday during the season, attracted wholesale buyers from Sligo, Londonderry and Newry and brought the Corporation a toll of 2d for every cask sold. Salted butter stored in wooden casks was shipped from these ports to England, mainly to Liverpool and Bristol. In the years 1832 and 1833 12,400 casks were exported. Fermanagh butter, almost incredibly, appears to have been exported to even more distant places.In 1834 the Ordnance Survey Memoirs note the objections raised about the materials used for making butter casks. Oak was the only material suitable for casks intended for Lisbon and the West Indies.

Trade links between Fermanagh and Scotland had also been established by 1834 and poultry and eggs were being exported to Glasgow. With the coming of the railway to Enniskillen in 1854, the export trade developed further. Live cattle and pigs, already exported in the 18th century, were now sent in large numbers to Belfast, Dundalk and Londonderry and shipped from there to Britain. A new export development in agricultural produce began in 1885 when the Scottish Co-operative Wholesale Society based in Glasgow, set up a buying depot in Enniskillen. Butter, eggs, fowl, pigs and fruit from rural Fermanagh were sent by rail and steamer to Glasgow, again through the ports of Londonderry and Belfast.

Most of the industries in Enniskillen in the 19th century catered for the local market. For example there was boot and shoe making, saddlery and harness making as adjuncts to the leather industry, and brewing and distilling used the locally grown corn.

By 1839 a directory of the towns of Sligo, Enniskillen, Ballyshannon and Donegal lists some 60 occupations in Enniskillen. Many continue today but over a quarter of that number are defunct. The black and whitesmiths, the brazier and brassfounder, cartwrights, coach and jaunting car makers, feather merchants, lastmakers, leather cutters, nailors, ropemakers, the skinner, straw-bonnet makers, tallow chandlers, tinsmiths, tanners, wheelwrights and the cutler are gone.

Some of these old crafts were renowned. The cutler, Richard Hurles, who came from Dublin in 1820, established his business in East Bridge Street and made cutlery not only for the local market but also for King William IV and Queen Victoria.

John C.Nixon, trained at Read's in Dublin as a sword, cutlery and surgical instrument maker, had come to Enniskillen in 1815 and was also established in East Bridge Street. Close by, in Belmore Street, the well known Enniskillen clockmaker Charles Oliver, operated in the late 18th century. He lived until 1822 and he trained a man by the name of McEntyre who succeeded him. Later in the 19th century there were fresh industries in Enniskillen which must have extended their markets beyond the Fermanagh area. John Canning's "Blacking Manufactory" in High Street produced "Real Irish Japan Liquid Paste Blacking"until his premises were destroyed by fire in 1849. In the 1860s 160 people were employed in McNeil's bobbin factory which had been set up by the Marquis of Ely in 1859 and 100 girls were employed in Galt's muslin factory in Henry Street and the ladies' cuffs and collars made there were exported to Manchester and London. Cassidy's tobacco factory was built in High Street in 1865 and employed 30 men making "Thick Twist", using pure Virginia tobacco imported via Liverpool.

In the 1830s there was an eel fishing industry situated about a mile below the town at Killyhevlin, where two eel weirs produced between 700 and 1000 dozen eels a year. Most were for local consumption, but some were salted and stored in casks.These were sent by water to Belturbet during the Lenten fasting period and retailed in Cavan and Longford.

The chief imports in 1834 were iron, coal, timber and slates, transported by water to Enniskillen from Ballyshannon. The same method had been used in 1790 to bring Portland stone to Enniskillen for the Earl of Belmore's new residence at Castle Coole. Earthenware was imported in the 1830s from Glasgow and Liverpool and during this period poultry and eggs were sent from Enniskillen to both ports.

The importation of timber and slates reflects the increase in building activity in the town. This had begun in the last decade

Above: This panoramic view from Windmill Hill to the south west shows the spire of the Church of Ireland Parish Church between the Methodist Church, built in 1865-67, and St Michael's Roman Catholic Church, completed in 1875. (Lawrence Coll. c.1880)

Opposite: View from the west taken from the Military Hospital on the Redoubt, c.1903. In the centre of the background in Wesley Street is the Methodist Church Hall of 1887 - the MacArthur Hall - with its distinctive traceried window. Nearby are the rooftops of Wellington Street, which in the early 19th century was the most fashionable residential area of the town, particularly for army officers. Apart from the man on the left, the figures in the foreground are soldiers of the Royal Inniskilling Fusiliers, those in the lighter colours wearing hospital uniforms. The seated figure in the centre is wearing a South African slouch or bush hat, probably brought back to Enniskillen after the Boer War in 1902. (Stereoscopic collection first published in New York in 1905)

of the 18th century when the threat of war with France impelled the Government to pour funds into defence work. The old Infantry Barracks near the Diamond gave way to an impressive Royal Barracks on the northwest of the island. Enniskillen Castle was refurbished as a barracks and work began on an extensive programme of barracks building which was to continue for the next thirty years.

Building activity also extended to projects other than military. A new county gaol was built in 1812-15, followed a few years later by the County Infirmary. A new town hall was completed in 1812 and in 1821-22 the 18th century court house was remodelled. In 1830 a corn market was built, followed a few years later by the butter market.

The population of Enniskillen increased dramatically in the 1820s. In 1821 it numbered 2,399; ten years later the figure was 6,056 and during the rest of the century it altered very little.

In 1834 the Ordnance Survey Memoirs record the prevailing diseases as rheumatism, consumption, dysentery and scurvy and note a rapid drop in the number of smallpox cases. Cholera, however was present with 212 cases recorded in the County Infirmary for 1832-33. The Union Workhouse was completed in 1845 for the relief of the poor and two years later was overcrowded with victims of the Famine. Epidemics of typhus and cholera followed and in 1849 the Fever Hospital was built.

The ecclesiastical buildings represent a wide variety of architectural styles. The oldest church, probably designed by William Farrell, is the Church of Ireland Parish Church, built in 1841 in a Perpendicular Gothic style on the site of a 17th century church. In 1924 it was elevated to the status of Cathedral. The Methodist Church has an imposing Classical facade and was designed in 1865 by W.J.Barre. St Michael's Roman Catholic Church was designed by O'Neill and Byrne in a 13th century Gothic style and was completed in 1875. The Presbyterian Church has a Gothic gabled front and was built in 1897. The Chapel of the Convent of Mercy is a neo-Byzantine building of 1904 designed by William Scott and is remarkable for its stained glass windows by Michael Healy, Lady Glenavy and Sarah Purser.

The early history of local government in Enniskillen is complex. From 1613 until 1840 it was in the hands of the Corporation. With the passing of the Municipal Reform Act of 1840, the Enniskillen Borough with a population of under 10,000, was dissolved and the control of the town passed temporarily to a Board of Guardians until Enniskillen Town Commissioners took control in 1846.In 1898 local government was reformed and from then until 1949 the town was administered by the Urban District Council. In 1949 Enniskillen reclaimed borough status and Enniskillen Borough Council replaced the Urban Council.

Enniskillen during the 19th century was a lively garrison town, gaining socially as well as financially from the regular influx of military personnel. In 1834 the Ordnance Survey Memoirs describe the main leisure pursuits as hunting, shooting, fishing, horse-racing, boat racing, sailing and cock fighting, the latter confined to the lower classes. Hunting included coursing with beagles.The boat racing included races for the distinctive Fermanagh 'cot' in which the peasantry could compete for prizes of between ten and twentyfive shillings.

Towards the end of the century, organised sport became popular and there was a tennis club, a polo club, a cricket club, football clubs, a golf club,and a hockey club, followed in the early years of the 20th century by Gaelic football and hurling under the auspices of the Gaelic Athletic Association.The Enniskillen Rowing Club Regatta was held every October, followed by the Regatta dinner in the Royal Hotel. In the early part of the century there had been a theatre in Schoolhouse Lane. Later, concerts, debates and theatrical events were held in the Town Hall and townspeople could promenade in the Forthill Park and listen to military bands.

In the early 19th century the people of Enniskillen had a reputation for being peaceable, high spirited and hospitable, although greatly opposed in their religious and political views. In 1846 the writer of the Parliamentary Gazetteer of Ireland commented on the superior dress of the inhabitants and the *opulence of the shops*. In 1834 most of the shopkeepers were newcomers to the town, rather than descendants of the original plantation settlers. They and the artisan classes are described in the Ordnance Survey Memoirs as *an intelligent people of sober habits* unlike the lower classes who are said to be *dissipated and immoral*, This view of the lower classes was not shared by Henry Inglis who toured Ireland in 1834 and found the lower classes of Enniskillen *by far the most respectable-looking* that he had seen in the whole country. He commented on the neatness of the women, none of them with *uncombed hair hanging about their ears* and was impressed by the *decent farmer-like appearance* of the men. He described in glowing terms the beauty of Enniskillen at harvest time:

On the sunny slopes that rise on all sides, the golden fields of ripe corn, were beautifully mingled with the brilliant green that follows the destruction of the meadow. Abundance of wood, and the broken surface of the country, gave sufficient shade to the landscape, which was, on all sides, imaged in the still, deep, broad waters that surround the town.

*Rowing gently on the river at the east end of the town. In 1954
the Queen Elizabeth Road was built along this river-side to
link up with the new Johnston Bridge. (Lawrence Coll.)*

The Castle Barracks and Castle Islands c.1885, with the rolling hills of Derrychara in the background. Throughout the 19th century Enniskillen was a bustling garrison town, its army population contributing substantially to the local economy. The river was used for transporting goods as well as for recreation and a row of steps by the river gave easy access for deliveries to the barracks. (Lawrence Coll,)

Built to house infantry in 1790, the Royal Military Barracks was designed by Mr Irvine of Derrygore. In 1834 it could accommodate over 600 soldiers and 95 horses; later it was enlarged to take 2000 soldiers and 224 horses. In 1936 it was converted at a cost of £50,000 into a training depot of the Royal Ulster Constabulary. (Lawrence Coll.)

No! Not a scout jamboree but yeomanry bell tents pitched on the slopes of Derrychara, c.1890. The east end of the town beyond the island is dominated by Cole's monument. On the right is the County Gaol. It was built in 1812-15 to a design of Richard Morrison and remained in use as a prison until 1901. On the left is the East Bridge and between the two is the gasworks run at this time by the Enniskillen Gas Company. Gas was first used to provide street lighting in the town in 1849, an occasion marked by a ceremony at the East Bridge where the first lamp was lit. Prior to that there were no street lights in Enniskillen. This state of affairs prompted Lieutenant Chaytor, officer of the Ordnance Survey to report in 1834, that in Enniskillen at night all one could hope for was **a faint gleam of a shop window** or **a dull lamp at the door of an inn.** (Lawrence Coll.)

*The East Bridge and the Island of **Inis Cethlenn** c.1880. In 1834 the bridge had five arches but only three remain today. and one of them is blocked with masonry. On the right is the Protestant Hall, built over a long period between 1850 and 1871. In the left background is the tall chimney of Bradshaw's steam saw mill. In the left foreground is **Inis Cethlenn**. The tradition that Enniskillen was named after this tiny islet was firmly believed by Lord Viscount Cole, who had the retaining wall built around it in 1831. His ancestor William Cole, founder of the town, is said to have planted a whitethorn bush on it and according to legend, if this tree died or disappeared, the Cole family would also move from Enniskillen. After the First World War the whitethorn died, at the time when the Cole family were selling off their interests in the town to their tenants. There are now no members of the family either in Enniskillen or in their family mansion of Florence Court.*

Thatched shops and houses in Belmore Street c.1895. On the left is William J. Davis' public house. The gas light over the door is advertising Guinness' Stout! In 1892 William Davis alias Davies took over the lease of the public house from Edward Shannon. This thoroughfare was originally called Gaol Street before being ennobled with the name of the Earls of Belmore of Castle Coole. (Crowder photograph)

In this photograph of c.1895, the quaint windows and half doors of these thatched houses in Old Henry Street, formerly John Street, peer apprehensively at their newly built stone neighbour - the Scottish Co-operative Wholesale Society. In 1837, out of a total of 1036 houses in Enniskillen, 375 were slated, the rest thatched.

*Townhall and East Bridge Street in the 1880s. On the left is the Belfast Banking Company (now the Northern Bank) an impressive palazzo style building of c.1880 probably designed by S.P. Close. Beside it is the **Gin Palace and Tea Warehouse**, a simple mid-Georgian building. Further down the street outside the Royal Hotel is Edward Monaghan's horse-drawn carriage. (Lawrence Coll.)*

PRESBYTERIAN CHURCH.ENNISKILLEN 1610, W.L.

The Presbyterian Church which formerly stood at the rear of East Bridge, c.1897. Built in 1827, it remained in use until 1897 when the present church was built further east in the same street. In the background is the Convent of Mercy. (Lawrence Coll.)

Busy High Street, c.1890, with horses and carts much in use. The Maguires of Alma House on the left - a drapery and haberdashery shop - claimed descent from the senior branch of the Maguire chieftains. Two doors below it is the drapery shop of W.R. Cooney, whose son Edward was founder of the Cooneyite religious movement, and two doors further down is Thomas Crowe's Family Grocery - the last thatched house in Enniskillen. (Lawrence Coll.)

A quiet stroll along Anne Street on a sunny afternoon c.1910 is interrupted by the noise of the newfangled "horseless carriage". Originally the whole street was called Darling Street after Edward Darling who obtained a lease of this area in 1717. The name Anne Street does not appear on an 1842 map by R.H. Frith but is recorded on the Ordnance Survey town map of 1858. (Lawrence Coll.)

The West Bridge c.1880-85. By 1825 the 18th century west bridge had become too narrow for the heavy traffic across it and a new bridge was designed and built in that year by J. McGuire at a cost of £2500. It remained in use until 1885 when it was replaced by the Erne bridge. A Lough Erne cot is moored midstream beside a cargo of wooden planks. The long building on the right is a brewery owned by Edward Brandon c.1802 and by Armstrong and Innis in 1839. By 1846 it was run by Armstrong and Jones and in 1877 it was purchased by W. and J. Downes. Ten years after this Downes added a mineral water factory to produce drinks still popular today such as lemonade, ginger ale and soda water along with others of less enduring popularity - sarsaparilla. seltzer, lithia water, kali and zoedone.

During the 1880s the Board of Works under the direction of its engineer James Price began a major drainage scheme of Lough Erne, a project - which had been the subject of numerous reports since the late 18th century. As part of this scheme the earlier three-arch bridge was replaced between 1885 and 1892 by this bridge - named the Erne bridge - and two deep channels were made in the river bed on either side of its central pier. This view of 1888 shows the river diverted around the north side of the island and the laborious work of clearing the river bed progressing well. 500 men were employed to do the work at a rate of 2/6 a day.

The 'back streets' between Queen Street and Hall's Lane c.1960-61. This area was cleared of houses in the late 1960s after its occupants were moved to new housing estates on the outskirts of the town. The first area to be occupied was Barrack, later Queen Street where houses were built in 1797. From 1825 the other streets were gradually developed, Strand Street, Head Street, Mary Street, Abbey Street, Dame Street, forming long terraced rows bounded by the back gardens of Darling Street on the south and on the east by an open area called Carleton's Park. By 1842 there was a National School at the corner of Head Street and Dame Street. By 1858 it had moved to Abbey Street and in 1905 the Sisters of Mercy took over this building and ran it as an infant school. (*Impartial Reporter* photograph)

Willoughby Place and The Brook in the 1920s or 1930s viewed through the former entrance to Portora Royal School. The houses of Willoughby Place were built between 1830 and 1841 and named after William Willoughby, the third Earl of

Enniskillen. The gun outside the gates of Portora was captured during the First World War and was melted down during World War 2.

There is a general air of prosperity in this busy scene showing High Street on a sunny day in 1901. Women are fashionably dressed, children well turned out. The empty tower niches on a newly built Townhall were shortly to be filled with the figures of an Inniskilling Dragoon and an Inniskilling Fusilier, to commemorate the two celebrated regiments of the town. (Lawrence Coll.)

White's Bookseller and Stationer in Townhall Street c.1880, with a good selection of picture postcards in the window and a range of baskets outside. The poster for **The Weekly News** advertises the news headlines of the day - including Home Rule, The Land Programme and the Knock Apparitions - all for one penny! Next door is Dr Obadiah Ternan's chemist shop distinguished by a fine wrought iron balcony.
(From a Lawrence photograph)

*The printing staff of **The Impartial Reporter,** c.1902, in their new printing works, built to replace the one destroyed by fire in 1901. In front is the foreman, James Preston. On his right is Gertie Fleming, who like the other women in the picture was a typesetter, and between them is Ned Mulligan, with directly behind him James Morrison, a later foreman. Also in the picture is Tommy Dorothy, second man from right. **The Impartial Reporter** newspaper was established in 1825 by William Trimble and John Gregston.*

The proprietors, Joseph and his sister Bridget Hackett stand between two members of staff outside their well stocked drapery shop in High Street in the 1920s. The sign in Irish reads **Mac Eoċaiḋ teac na n-earraide ndeas** - Hackett, house of nice merchandise.

W. R. Wilson's chemist shop at 39 Darling Street, (now number 17) c.1900. In December 1900 W. S. Taylor acquired Wilson's shop and set up a chemist shop there for a time before moving to Townhall Street. Much of this attractive shop front is still retained today in Elliott's Grocery Shop.

*Inside Taylor's Pharmaceutical Chemist shop in Townhall
Street in the 1920s. The main promotion of the day appears to
be* **Health Salt.**

Matthew Campbell in the doorway of his new and second hand clothes shop in East Bridge Street, c.1910. Later his son set up a barber's shop in the adjoining house and his grandson James, also a barber, occupied the two houses until recently.

These houses are among the oldest in the town , and one of them was the premises of the cutler Richard Hurles, who came to Enniskillen in 1820. After his death in 1862, one of his apprentices continued the cutlery business for a time.

John O'Donnell in the doorway of his butcher's shop at number 1 Water Street, c.1900.

Two of the Maguire brothers and a young boy pose in front of their forge in Gas Lane at the east end of town. The Maguires were whitesmiths as well as blacksmiths and their working day was long. Repairing bicycles, including here a penny farthing, was obviously an important part of their business at this time (1880-90).

The forerunner of the Scottish Co-operative Wholesale Society? In c.1895 this small sales outlet for eggs was located in Victoria Terrace, The Brook, on the road to Belleek. (Possibly a Lawrence photograph)

Horses were still used to transport goods locally in the 1930s and the work of the blacksmith was important both in town and country. Here David Blair shoes a cart horse in 1930 at his forge in Forthill Street, which he continued to operate until the 1950s. (Photograph by Jack Somerville)

Thomas Craigmile, carter for Enniskillen Urban District Council, outside Blair's forge in Forthill Street in 1927. In those days street sweepers had the job of gathering the town's refuse to the side of the road. It was then collected by the carter who brought it to the dump at the Broad Meadow. (Photograph by David Blair)

A display of turkeys at the Scottish Co-operative Wholesale Society on the Sligo road in 1939. Lily Henderson and Josie Feely are at work earning extra money plucking turkeys for the Christmas market. They were paid 6d for plucking a turkey, 3d for a chicken.

The Scottish Co-operative Wholesale Society on the Sligo road. The S.C.W.S. started business in Glasgow in 1868 and in 1885 set up a buying depot in Enniskillen, providing important employment in the area. The main products collected were butter, eggs and pigs, and in the season fruit and fowl. A small creamery was also established, as well as eight auxiliary creameries within a few miles of the town. The products were transported by rail and steamer to Glasgow through the ports of Londonderry and Belfast. These buildings with their unusual "Dutch" gables were designed in 1893 by Thomas Elliot, church architect of Enniskillen (1833-1915). "Thistle House" in the foreground, was built for William Whyte, the first manager of the Society. (Lawrence Coll.)

Enniskillen Market House is bedecked with flags to mark the Diamond Jubilee of Queen Victoria's reign in 1897. The Jubilee was celebrated on June 24th with band parades, bonfires and sports events. In the same year a Jubilee wing was added to the County Infirmary, proper drains were laid and coal fires and gas lighting were installed. (Dundas Collection)

Official public announcements such as this proclamation in 1910 of the accession of King George V were formally made outside Enniskillen Court House. The man in the centre reading the proclamation is the High Sheriff, J. C. Johnston of **Magherameena.** *Behind him to the left is Viscount Corry D. L., the Town Clerk, Arthur Ritchie stands in front seventh from left and the mace bearer is the Town Sergeant, James Slavin. In the foreground is a detachment from the Hampshire Regiment under Lieutenant Lidley. On the right is District Inspector Armstrong who led a Guard of Honour from the Royal Irish Constabulary. At the end of the reading came the royal salute and the unfurling of the Union Jack. The people sang God Save the King and then at the call of E. M. Archdale, three cheers were given for the King, George V and the ceremony came to an end. Among those who attended the ceremony were Captain and Adjutant A. D. Best; Major D'Arcy Irvine; J. Porter Porter, D. L; Major Haire; G. Massey Beresford, D. L.; R. Sparrow, R. M.; W. R. Cooney, J. P.; W. G. Henderson, J. P. and W. Copeland Trimble, J. P. (back, right side, on Court House steps). (Photograph by Mercer)*

The junior drawing class of Portora Royal School concentrates
on geometrical and other shapes on an afternoon in 1896.
(Photograph by Robert Welch)

Presentation Brothers School, early 20th century. In 1899 the Presentation Brothers took over the running of the St Michael's Primary School near the East Bridge, a Catholic boy's school formerly staffed by Christian Brothers from at least 1858 until the order left Enniskillen in 1897. They also ran a Secondary School nearby. (See page 56)

Pupils of Enniskillen Girls Model School c. 1916. The Headmistress Mrs Anne Kathleen Rice is in the middle row on the right, and the rector of Enniskillen Parish Church, Canon Webb, is in the centre. The girls have just taken part in the ceremony of crowning Ethel Crawford as May Queen. During this event, held every year during the last week in April, Tennyson's May Queen was memorised and the Queen and her Maids of Honour wore wreaths and garlands of fresh spring flowers. Enniskillen Model School opened in 1867 with 3 departments for boys, girls and infants, and the pupils were drawn from both Protestant and the Catholic communities. It had accommodation for 400 pupils and a residence for the Headmaster and eight pupil teachers. In 1923 the Boys' School and Girls' School were amalgamated and these amalgamated with the Infants' School in 1937. (Photograph by Mercer)

Lord Ashbourne (1868-1942) (back row) prominent supporter of the Gaelic League, poses with pupils of the Convent of Mercy, winners of the Ashbourne shield, in 1936. Mount Lourdes was the first girls' school to receive this trophy, presented by Lord Ashbourne for achievement in spoken Irish. Lord Ashbourne normally wore a kilt and cloak and on this occasion the pupils also were clad in Irish costume for the performance of a play in Irish **Faoi brat na Saoirse** (Under the cloak of Freedom) written by a Dublin teacher Aine Cannon. The Sisters of Mercy started a secondary girls school in 1909 and eight years later moved into a new building - the first Mount Lourdes.

Members of the cavalry of Volunteer Enniskillen Horse assemble outside the former County Gaol c.1912-13. The regiment was hastily formed in 1912 to escort Sir Edward Carson in Enniskillen where he began his Ulster campaign against Home Rule. The Commanding Officer William Copeland Trimble stands in front at the centre. His second in command, Edward Kerr stands on the extreme left. The central building in the background housed the administrative section of the prison. When the gaol closed it gave access to the new Technical School, opened in 1990 in the former prison hospital and to the County Hall housed in a prison cell block. The Technical School founded under the Agriculture and Technical Instruction (Ireland) Act of 1899 accounts for the sign "County Fermanagh Art and Industrial Development" over the entrance building. The attached building on the left was used by the Ministry of Labour and the one on the right was for a short period the Victoria Hotel before becoming a barracks for the Royal Irish Constabulary.

Sir Edward Carson being driven through the town in a horse drawn carriage on September 18th 1912. The large building in the background housing Betty's shop and the Y.M.C.A. hall was later removed. This widened the existing alleyway to form the Regal Pass. Earlier the Primitive Methodists' preaching house had stood on the Y.M.C.A. site.

Onlookers at the Gaol Square watch the parade of Enniskillen Horse on Easter Monday 1913. The large building in the left background is the County Infirmary built by the architect James Downes in 1917. In November 1914 after the outbreak of war, the Enniskillen Horse became the Service Squadron of the Inniskilling Dragoons and was absorbed into the 36th Ulster Division.

The Colours of the 2nd Battalion of the Royal Inniskilling Fusiliers being taken from St Macartin's Cathedral in 1952 after being handed over by H.R.H. the Duke of Gloucester. On *the same day the Regiment received the Freedom of the Borough.*

Remembrance ceremony at the War Memorial in Belmore Street between World War 1 and World War 2. This was erected in memory of those killed in the First World War and now also commemorates the dead of World War 2. The bronze figure of the soldier with bowed head and arms reversed - so much a symbol of the suffering of Enniskillen in the bombing tragedy of 1987 - is the work of a relatively unknown English sculptor called Gaffin. In the background is St Michael's Primary School on the left, St Michael's Secondary School in the centre and behind it the Sisters of Mercy Convent and School.

The first wreath-laying ceremony at the War Memorial took place on October 25th 1922. Laying the wreath is James Baker, in memory of his uncle, James Edward Malone, who had served with the Royal Inniskilling Fusiliers in France. The boy beside him, about to lay flowers, is Vincent McCaffrey. This important occasion was marked by the attendance of the last Lord Lieutenant of Ireland, Lord Wimbourne.

Illuminated shrine set up in Enniskillen at the National Foresters' Hall as part of Fermanagh's celebration of the Eucharistic Congress - a large scale religious festival held in Dublin from June 10th-17th, 1932. From left are Gerald Healy, Charles McKeown, Johnnie McCullion, William Blake and Seamus Whittaker, then a student for the priesthood.

*Cahir Healy, poet, writer and a leader of the northern nationalist movement, in the 1920s. As a young man, Healy had worked as a journalist with the **Fermanagh News** and a number of western newspapers before settling in Enniskillen as an insurance supervisor about 1900. After his efforts to prevent partition failed, he pushed the case, again unsuccessfully, for strong nationalist counties like Tyrone and Fermanagh to be included in the south. He died in 1970 and is remembered for his tolerant, non-sectarian view of Irish nationalism. (Photograph by Lafayette of Dublin)*

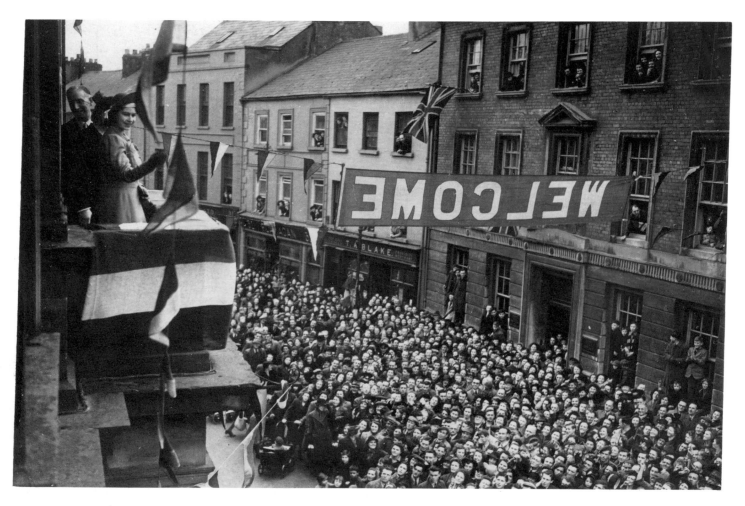

A warm welcome greeted H.R.H. Princess Elizabeth on her visit to Enniskillen on March 19th 1946. Accompanying the Princess on the balcony of the Townhall is the chairman of the Urban District Council William E. Johnstown. The Princess was greeted with loud cheering, the peeling of bells from the Cathedral followed by the National Anthem played by the band of the Royal Ulster Rifles 1st Battalion.
*(**Belfast Telegraph** photograph)*

On April 29th 1949 Enniskillen became a Municipal Borough again. The mace belonging to the earlier Corporation is examined here by the Governor of Northern Ireland, Lord Granville, in the presence of (from left) William E. Johnston, the new Mayor; Sir Basil Brooke, Prime Minister; and Noble Connor Johnston, Town Clerk.

Opposite: *Coursing on Devenish Island in 1837, and a relaxed day out for the family. (Print by J.H. Burgess)*

Above: *Coursing continued to be a popular sport in the 1930s. Here dogs are paraded by T.F. Campbell (on left) and Gerard Healy (on right) for an American visitor. (Photograph by William Hudson)*

An enthusiastic line-up of bicyclists assembles at the Gaol Square on June 24th 1897 to take part in the town's Diamond Jubilee celebrations. In the 1890s there were regular cycling excursions organised by the Enniskillen Cycling Club. In the background is the railway station adorned with flags and bunting. (Dundas Collection)

Players and supporters in the 1880s at Enniskillen Lawn Tennis Club grounds, which were situated on or near the Broad Meadow, at the rear of the Ulster Bank. The club was formed prior to 1882, for in January of that year the club's minute book records a committee meeting in the Town Hall at which members decided to raise the subscription from 5/- to 10/-. The club moved to more commodious grounds in 1907 behind Alexandra Terrace (Photograph by Mercer)

The Ashwoods Maguires Hurling Team in 1905. The "Ashwoods Maguires" were formed in April 1903 by Arthur Fee and their playing pitch was at Drumawill on the outskirts of Enniskillen. They won the Fermanagh Senior Hurling Championship in 1905 and again in 1908. The members of the team are, from left: **Front row:** *Albert Wilson, Thomas Slevin, Joseph Smyth holding the championship cup, Charles Cassidy, and Charles Carleton.* **Middle row:** *Robert Dooris, Pat Carleton, Joseph Hussard, William Smith and Edward McCaffrey.* **Back row:** *Pat McCaffrey, Connie McManus, Thomas Keys, William McGloin, John Cassidy, Hugh McManus, Pat Slevin, William Lunny and Peter Cassidy. (Photograph probably by Thomas Walsh)*

Members of the Co. Fermanagh polo team after winning the **Inter-County Challenge in 1882.** *From left: A. F. Maude, E. M. Archdale, The Earl of Erne, C. C. D'Arcy Irvine and the captain J. Porter Porter. Prior to 1910 the polo horses were stabled at Drumadravy, Lisnarick, originally an Archdale dower house, and at one time the polo pitch was at St Angelo. (Photograph by Mercer)*

The Celtic soccer football team of Enniskillen 1902-03. From **left front:** *Joe O'Donnell, Jim Irvine, John McKeown, Ginger Husbands, Ned Smith.* **Centre:** *Frank Husbands, Danny Maguire, John Holmes.* **Back:** *J. Doherty, P. Donnelly, B. Nolan, T. Gibson, J. Gillen, Barney Skiffington, E. Maguire, T. Bradley, F. Hynes. (Photograph probably by Mercer)*

*Enniskillen Hockey Team 1903. Standing **from left:** W. E. Trimble, H. C. Gordon, Captain Morris, S. C. Clarke, J. Smith, C. McDonagh, T. Orr, unidentified. Seated **from left:** J. Mercer, Tracey, T. M. Crowe (captain of the team), S. F. Griffith and F. Thorpe. (Photograph probably by Mercer)*

Racing four from Portora Royal School training on the River Erne, c.1910. The heyday of the boat club was from 1904 when the headmaster A.C. MacDonnell introduced or re-introduced formal rowing, until the outbreak of war in 1914. During that time crews from Portora rowed regularly at open regattas in other clubs as far afield as Trinity, Boyne, Derry and Portadown. In 1915 the club suffered a setback when a disastrous gale destroyed its boats and boathouse. In the background is the school. The main block was built in 1777, the colonnades and wings added in 1837-8 and further additions were built behind the colonnades in 1859-61. (Lawrence Coll.)

Portora cricket team of 1923. Seated on the right is Samuel Beckett, the celebrated writer (1903-1989) who from 1920-1923 during his school days at Portora distinguished himself at several sports. The other members of the team are from left, **back:** *R. E. Hemphill, S.H.M. Webb, A. P. Webb, E. G. Fitt and C.H.H. Swiney;* **middle:** *E.P.C. Woods, C. M. (later Sir Colville) Deverell, C. P. (later General Sir Charles) Jones and A. Percy Harris.* **Seated on left:** *A. G. Thompson, in centre A. McM. Buchanan.*

Music making in seclusion in the drawing room of Portora Royal School. This photograph may date to the period 1891-4 when Dr Lindsey was headmaster of Portora. The photo-grapher and her family lived beside the school and were particularly friendly with the Lindsey family. (Photograph by Annie King)

Afternoon tea in the garden c. 1891-4. This photograph may have been taken in the grounds of Portora. The photographer's mother Mrs Anna Haire King is on the right and the others are probably Mrs Lindsey and her children. (Photograph by Annie King)

A tug of war c. 1909. In the centre, fourth from the left is Edith Kidd, whose father Leonard Kidd was Chief Surgeon in charge of the County Infirmary (renamed the County Hospital in the 1920s) from 1897 until 1937.

*The band of the Boys Brigade entertains a large crowd at a fete on Forthill in 1946, probably to celebrate the end of the War. The Forthill - so called after the 17th century earthen fort on its summit - was earlier called Camomile Hill. Until 1832 it was a commons where the people of Enniskillen had grazing rights. Then it was enclosed and planted to provide a park for the public. The bandstand was erected in 1895 in honour of Thomas Plunkett, who as chairman of the Town Commissioners from 1882-85 and 1888-94 had been responsible for turning the park into one of the most beautiful pleasure grounds in the country. (**Belfast Telegraph** photograph)*

William Scott (front right) and his band c. 1895. William Scott (1865-1910) is remembered as the woodcarver responsible for the ornate doors of Enniskillen townhall and the stalls in the Convent of Mercy Chapel. His business premises were in Darling Street. However during his lifetime he was best known as an exceptionally versatile musician, accomplished in singing as well as in playing violin, cello, dulcimer, xylophone, banjo and guitar. His band included his uncle James Connor (second from left) and one or possibly two members of the Ritchie family. They played regularly at local entertainments and concerts. (Photograph by Crowder)

*In 1910 The Enniskillen Temperance Dramatic Society staged Boucicault's play **The Shaughran**. The cast included Alderman Charles McKeown (third from left) who played the part of Con. The production was staged in St Michael's Boys Primary School and the costumes were hired in Edinburgh.*

Festive dance at the townhall c. 1925. The lady in white at the centre is Miss Dorothy Falls. On the far left Mrs Pakenham of Blaney stands next to Mrs Gerard Irvine of Killadeas.

Fun in fancy dress at Killadeas House, now the Manor House Hotel, in 1925. Seated in the front is Miss Eileen Gerrity and standing in the front of the car is Miss Rita Kidd.

Lady of the Lake moored at Enniskillen c.1900. Advertised in 1897 as a new paddle steamer, the **Lady of the Lake** was in fact the renovation of an older vessel, the **P.S. Rossclare** built by Lewis and Stockwell of London and run by H.M. Darcy Irvine for about four years from 1866 to ferry passengers to and from his new hotel at Rossclare, near Killadeas. From 1896 to 1915 the **Lady of the Lake** linked up with the Sligo, Leitrim and Northern Counties and Great Northern railway companies to provide an excellent tourist service in the area. It was also much used by local people for picnic outings to various islands in Lough Erne. For £1 the whole family was entitled to unlimited travel throughout the summer. (Photograph by Annie King)

*An excursion party - possibly members of the Belfast Naturalists Field Club - on board the **Lady of the Lake** c. 1985. At the centre in front, wisely armed with an umbrella is William Copeland Trimble of Enniskillen (1851-1941), proprietor of **The Impartial Reporter** and author of the **History of Enniskillen.** (Photograph by Robert Welch)*

*Tourists on board the S. S. **Belturbet** c. 1890. The S. S.*
***Belturbet** built at Preston in 1880, was owned by J. Grey Vesey*
Porter of Belleisle. It was used mainly for tourist excursions,
with entertainment provided on board by Porter's Belleisle
Brass Band. After Porter's death it was sold to the Erne Yacht
Club and was used as a house boat until it was sold for scrap
during the First World War. (Lawrence Coll.)

Upper Lough Erne was also popular for boat trips. The tranquillity of the lake is captured in this view of a motorboat near Gadd Island c. 1900. James Eadie is at the stern and his companion *is probably a member of the Henderson family. In the background is a small steamboat. (Photograph by W. G. Eadie)*

One of the most frequently visited islands in Lower Lough Erne was Devenish, with its round tower and monastic ruins. Here a party sets out to row to the island.

The Board of Guardians of the Union Workhouse employed a ferryman to row officials, medical staff and clergy from the end of Market Street across the river to the Workhouse, thus avoiding a long journey by way of Mill Street. The ferryman in this view of c.1900 is Mr Feely and the large building nearest the shore is the Fever Hospital opened in 1849. The Workhouse building in the background, designed by George Wilkinson, was started in 1841 and opened at the end of 1845. The scene of much suffering during the famine years, it finally closed in 1948. (Dundas Collection)

Both the Imperial and the Royal Hotels provided horse-drawn carriages to convey guests to and from the railway station. Here the carriage from the Royal Hotel heads towards the station. The Royal Hotel was opened in 1865 by Edward Monaghan, who had worked as a driver on the Bianconi Coach between Enniskillen and Sligo. (From a Lawrence photograph, c.1910)

From c.1906 to c. 1950 this horse drawn wagonette was used to transport pupils from the areas of Bellanaleck, Cleenish and Drumany to the original Jones Memorial parish school at Lisgoole. It was provided by Archdeacon Pratt, rector of Rossorry parish, to counter objections by parents in the Bellanaleck area to the closing of their small school in the village. This photograph was taken outside the gates of Lisgoole Abbey c.1910 by Thomas Walsh.

Above: The staff of the Imperial Hotel pose for this photograph taken in 1901-02. The progressive character of the hotel with its Swiss manager is suggested by the new mode of transport - the motor car - parked outside, with the horse-drawn hotel carriage very much in the background. The hotel was established about 1840 by William Robert Armstrong. The picture borrows the clock tower and portico of the Town Hall to add its opulence! It was photographed by E. Goetz and printed as a postcard in Lucerne.

Opposite: All eyes are on this early Daimler car in the Hollow, Enniskillen in 1901-02. The car was jointly owned by the photographer and his brother James Eadie, seen here at the wheel. It has no number plates; these were not introduced until 1903. (Photograph by W. G. Eadie)

*Railway employees at Enniskillen Station in 1937. Among those identified are: **Back row:** Tommy Woods, on left, Joe Smith, George Britton, third from left, Billy Noble, Tommy Palmer and Jack Ellis. **Middle row:** H. Grey, G. Ramsey, Ned Flanagan, Mr Clarke and Billy McIntyre. **Front row:** Jack Reid. Mr Henderson, W. McIntyre, Miss L. Troughton, fourth from right, Mr Russell, Chief Clerk, third from right, Miss Howard second from right and George Robinson.*

Cornelius Templeman in front of Jack Cousins, setting off for Bundoran on a Sunday excursion from Enniskillen Station c. 1928. (Photograph by David Blair)

The Weirs bridge at Killyhevlin, c.1915. So called from two former eel weirs on the site, it was built by Courtney, Stephens and Bailey of Dublin in 1878-9 to carry the Sligo, Leitrim and Northern Counties Railway across the river Erne. The S. L. and N. C. R. ran from the Great Northern station at Enniskillen to the Midland Great Western Railway near Ballisodare in Sligo. It conveyed both goods and passengers and took more than three hours to travel from Enniskillen to Sligo. In 1934 a swimming pool was made beside the bridge and became the focus for a thriving swimming club. The bridge was taken down in the early 1960s after the closing of the railway in 1957.

Enniskillen Railway Station was built in 1858-9 to a design of William George Murray for the Dundalk and Enniskillen Railway. When the first train arrived in Enniskillen from Dundalk in 1859, the Russian gun on Forthill, captured during the Crimean War, was fired in salute and all the windows in Belmore Street were broken. Later, in 1876, the Dundalk and Enniskillen Railway became part of the Great Northern Railway and this photograph was taken in December 1957, shortly after the closing of the line. Thackeray visited Enniskillen in the summer of 1842, before the days of the railway. He left us this pen picture of an early morning in the town: *Goodby, moreover, neat Enniskillen, over the bridge and churches whereof the sun peepeth as the coach starteth from the inn.*" (**The Irish Sketch-Book**) **(Belfast Telegraph)**

THE PHOTOGRAPHERS

Annie King c. 1895

These photographs have been drawn from the work of about thirty photographers, half of whom it is possible to name. The earliest was George Crowder, who had a studio in Willoughby Place, Enniskillen in 1867-8. Later he moved to the town centre, and he was still there, at 26 Townhall Street, towards the end of the century. He also had a studio in Bundoran, where his wife ran a successful cafe. At that time, Bundoran was, in the words of the antiquarian Wakeman, "the most fashionable watering-place in the north-west of Ireland" and a Mecca for the professional photographer.

Photographs from the Lawrence collection are well represented, with sixteen photographs, all probably the work of the remarkable Dublin photographer Robert French, who joined the photographic firm of William Lawrence in the 1860s. The earliest dates to about 1880, although earlier Lawrence views of the town exist, including stereoscopic photographs. These twin images taken with a double lensed camera gave a three dimensional effect when looked at through a special viewer. They were very fashionable in Ireland from the 1850s until the later 1870s. French came frequently to Enniskillen from 1880 until the First World War, updating his subjects as changes occurred, usually placing the camera in exactly the same position as before.

Five photographs can definitely be attributed to the photographer T.A.Mercer who established a photographic studio and jewellery shop in the centre of Enniskillen in 1881. For the next forty years he provided a wide ranging service in Fermanagh including landscape, architectural, group and equestrian photography as well as studio portraits, either in monochrome or finished in oil or watercolour.

There are two photographs by the celebrated Strabane born photographer Robert Welch. At a young age he received his first lessons in photography in Enniskillen where his Scottish father, David, ran a successful photographic business in Victoria Terrace, near Willoughby Place from 1865 until 1868. David Welch photographed many of the historic sites in Fermanagh and received recognition as official photographer to the Lord Lieutenant and to the Marquis of Hamilton, later Duke of Abercorn.

The work of another professional photographer, William Hudson, is also represented. Hudson, a native of Bury in Lancashire, spent some years in Strabane before setting up his studio in Belmore Street, Enniskillen in 1912 or 1913. Later he moved his Enniskillen studio to Darling Street. He was in his eighties when he died in 1959 and his son, Harry, continued the business until his death in 1977.

Other professional photographers are represented. The postcard view of the Imperial Hotel, Townhall Street, printed in Lucerne about 1902, was the work of E. Goetz; Lafayette of Dublin and various photographers from the *Belfast Telegraph*.

Among the amateurs, the best known is Annie King (c.1864-1920) who lived at 36 Willoughby Place in Enniskillen and captured in her photographs the tranquil life of the more leisured classes.

W.G.Eadie of Snowhill, was another gifted amateur photographer who produced work of remarkable quality. He was chairman of Henderson and Eadie's Woollen Mill in Lisbellaw and was also a pioneer of motoring.

The photographs from Canon Dundas' collection were selected more for their historic interest than their visual impact.They may have been taken by Canon Dundas himself, who was a noted local historian and the author of an important history of Enniskillen, published in 1913.

Other local photographers are Thomas Walsh of Culkey and David Blair who formerly lived in Belmore Street, Enniskillen. Walsh, who succeeded his father in running Lisgoole Bridge Garden Nursery, took a keen interest in photography for a short time in his youth. A few of his prints, dating to around 1910 have survived, but, unfortunately, none of his glass-plate negatives. David Blair's photographs were taken with a simple Brownie Camera. He had a forge in Forthill Street where he worked for many years as a general jobbing smith and horse shoer. His photographs were taken mainly in the 1920 s and provide an unusual record of life at the east end of Enniskillen. Sadly, David Blair died in May 1990, while this book was in preparation.

ACKNOWLEDGMENTS

I would like to record my warm thanks to those who lent prints and photographs and provided information (page references in brackets): His Honour Judge R. Babington, (47), The Earl of Belmore, (10,62), Mrs Lana Bridger, (76), Mr James Campbell, (38,40,63), Mr John Deering, (36,37), Mr Roland Eadie, (83,39), Mr Pete Healy, (59), Mrs Colette Henderson, (39), Miss Rita Kidd, (74,78,79), Mrs May Kilpatrick, (90), Mrs Breege McCusker, (92), Mr Cahir McKeown, (58), the Trustees of Portora Royal School, (48,71), the Sisters of Mercy, Enniskillen, (51), Major George Stephens and The Royal Inniskilling Fusiliers Museum, (55) Mr Joe Towner, (44), Miss Joan Trimble, (6,22,34,52,54), and Miss Lilas Walsh, (66,87).

My thanks are also due to those who have contributed to the photographic archives of Fermanagh County Museum and to Fermanagh District Council for allowing me access to these archives: Mr James Baker, (57), Mr David Blair, (42, 43, 91), Mr Walter Brady, (26,32), Mr C. Carson (50), Mr Pat Cassidy and Mr Maguire, (49), Mr John Deering and Mr George Balfour, (35,65,81), Mr Noble Connor Johnston, (56,61,75), Miss Rita Kidd, (24), Miss Mary Lowans, (72,73,80), Mr John McCabe, (14,17, 18,24,25,27,30,33,45,60,45, 86,93), Mr Cahir McKeown, (68,77), Mrs Pat O'Connor, (53), Mr Egbert Trimble, (23,28,41), Miss Joan Trimble, (69), and Mrs Hilary Wright, (for the Dundas Collection).

The Lawrence photographs are reproduced by kind permission of the National Library of Ireland and permission to reproduce prints and photographs has also been kindly given by the National Museum of Ireland, (4), the Belfast Telegraph, (60,75,93), and the Queen's University of Belfast, (8,15).

I am also indebted to others who helped me in my researches: Mr Acheson Aiken, Mr Gabriel Brock, Mr Richard Bennett, Mr Joseph Carleton, Miss Aideen Ireland, Mr Frank Kerrin, Mrs Bernadette Layden, Father McCarney, Mr Leo McCarney, Dr Harmon Murtagh, Mr Shay Nethercott,

Mr Robert Northridge, Mr J. O'Neill, Mr David Phair, Mr Desmond Preston and the staff of Enniskillen Library, in particular Mrs Mariana Maguire, Mr Frankie Roofe, Sisters M. Aquinas, Consilii and Eucharia, Miss Sheila Slevin and Mr Mervyn Winslow.

Special thanks must be given to two Enniskilleners, John McCabe and Joan Trimble, who kindly read my typescript, offered me much advice and generously gave me the benefit of their great knowledge of the history of Enniskillen. I am also much indebted to my editors Dr Brian Mercer Walker and Mrs Margaret McNulty. Finally I would like to thank my former colleague Iain Macaulay and my daughter Nora Hickey for initiating me into the wonders of word processing and my husband Philip Wood for much helpful discussion.

FURTHER READING

Enniskillen has been well served by its historians and there are many good histories of the town, most, unfortunately, difficult to obtain. The earliest is *Enniskillen Long Ago* by W.H. Bradshaw published in 1878, followed by *Enniskillen, Parish and Town* by W.H. Dundas, Dundalk, 1913, and between 1919-21 in Enniskillen, Trimble's comprehensive *History of Enniskillen* in three volumes. Many of the general books about Fermanagh contain information about Enniskillen including Reverend William Henry's *Upper Lough Erne* 1739 (reprinted 1987), W.F. Wakeman's *Lough Erne* 1870, Enniskillen and Dublin, Peadar Livingstone's *The Fermanagh Story* 1969, Enniskillen, and Mary Rogers' *Prospect of Erne* 1967, Belfast and *Prospect of Fermanagh* 1982, Enniskillen. There is also a very comprehensive bibliography in *The Fermanagh Story*. More recently Hugh Dixon's *In the Town of Enniskillen* 1973, Ulster Architectural Heritage Society, Belfast, provides a thorough architectural survey of the town, the Kilmacormick W.E.A. History Group's *A Dander down the Streets* 1988, Belfast, a social history of the "back streets" community of Enniskillen and Gabriel Brock's *The Gaelic Athletic Association in Co. Fermanagh* 1984, Monaghan, a detailed account of Gaelic sport in Fermanagh.

There are many useful articles in the *Clogher Record* including those by Dr D.B.McNeill on public transport in Fermanagh (1982, 1983, 1984), by Robert J. Hunter on Sir William Cole and plantation Enniskillen (1978), by Jean Agnew on social life in Enniskillen a century ago (1967) and by Catherine McCullough (1988) on manufacturing and trading in Enniskillen.

Among the primary sources are T.C. Yates and Thomas R. Mould's *Report on the Town of Enniskillen: with a Description of the Proposed Boundary*, 1832, the *Report on the Borough of Enniskillen by the Commissioners on Municipal Corporations in Ireland*, 1833-34 and the Ordnance Survey Memoirs, 1834 (publication forthcoming). Also worth consulting are the various trade directories, Pigot and Co.'s *Directory of Ireland*, 1846, 1856, 1881, Macloskie's *Handbook for the County of Fermanagh*, 1848, *Belfast and Ulster Directory*, 1863-64, Lowe's *Fermanagh Directory and Household Almanac*, 1879 (reprint 1990), Porter's *Guide*, 1909, and *Belfast and Ulster Trades Directory*, 1926.